How to Dry Flowers the Easy Way

Audrey Steiner Bugbee

How to Dry Flowers
the Easy Way

with photographs by
John Murphy and Timothy Cross

Houghton Mifflin Company, Boston
1975

H 10 9 8 7 6 5 4 3 2 1

Library of Congress Cataloging in Publication Data

Bugbee, Audrey Steiner.
  How to dry flowers the easy way.

  1. Flowers—Drying. I. Title.
SB447.B83   745.92   74–30113
ISBN 0–395–20441–0

Printed in the United States of America

To Harry, for his constant encouragement,
and to my granddaughters, Valerie and Kathryn,
that they may have something other
than possessions from me

With great appreciation to Frances Tenenbaum,

my editor, for her invaluable guidance,

and to John Murphy and Timothy Cross,

my photographers

Contents

Part Three: Special Projects

Introduction

Some measure time by stars,
And some by hours;
Some measure days by dreams,
And some by flowers . . .

— *Madison Julius Cawein*

THE DESIRE to preserve flowers in their natural beauty is probably universal. As a child, I spent many happy hours with my Swiss grandmother in her old-fashioned garden, and I still remember feeling a pang of sorrow at the sight of a wilting blossom. At least some of my pleasure in drying flowers must come from the illusion that I am extending their normal life span.

What started me on flower-drying as a hobby, though, was nothing quite that sentimental. For many years my husband and I have collected eighteenth-century furniture, mostly Pennsylvania German pieces brought to Ohio and other Middle Western states by westward-migrating families. On a visit to Williamsburg, I was impressed by the dried-flower arrangements for which the Restoration is famous, and particularly with how beautifully they complemented the eighteenth-century rooms.

Although several times before, I had thought it would

be fun to learn flower-drying, I had always given up because I couldn't seem to find a simple, straightforward instruction book for beginners. This time, however, I determined to figure it out for myself. I tried all different kinds and combinations of flower-drying materials and discovered that I could use just two simple ones, sand and air, and obtain perfectly satisfactory results — results, that were better, in fact, than those I achieved with more expensive, difficult, or unpleasant materials.

I found that many precise or tedious rules didn't have to be followed. Flowers dried in sand or air don't have to be timed, for example. If the flowers weren't completely dry when I first removed them from the sand, they could simply be re-covered and left to dry longer. If they were left too long, they didn't fade or "burn." I picked flowers and dried them whenever I felt like it, instead of at a particular time of day or stage of their development, and again found this to work very well.

As I experimented, I kept copious notes for my own reference. Later, as my arrangements began to be seen — particularly those I had included in an exhibit of our furniture in the Toledo Museum of Art — and people began to ask me how they could learn to dry flowers, the notes became the basis for this book.

Clearly, my method is not the only way to dry flowers. I don't even argue that it is necessarily the best one for every purpose and every person. But it is fun, it requires little or no expense or equipment and, above all, it is easy to learn. Because of this, it can be learned and enjoyed by virtually anyone of any age — busy people and those who have much time on their hands. If it brings pleasure to many people, it will bring an added measure to me.

Part I

Basic Techniques

Sand

Storage and drying boxes. The most useful are shoe
boxes, blouse and shirt boxes, dress and suit
boxes, stationery boxes — and the containers
from all the cottage cheese your family can eat.
Be sure not to throw away the box tops, because
although you *dry* your material uncovered, you
store it in closed boxes

Eyebrow tweezers

A pair of small wire clippers

A pair of small scissors with good sharp points

An artist's paintbrush — small and fine

A plastic bucket or a large bowl to hold your sand

Eight-ounce paper cups for pouring sand

Wire coat hangers for air-drying

Five packages of pipe cleaners and any kind of
string, for hanging air-dried material

Florist's wire in sizes 18, 22, and 26. You will use
these to add stems and support flower heads.
They cost about a penny apiece at a florist shop
or garden center. (In case they don't come num-
bered where you buy them, the *lower* numbers
are heavier than the higher ones. With a bit of
experience, you won't have any problem figuring
out which wire is most suitable for your purpose)

Green florist's tape to cover the wire. Buy a small
roll because it dries out if it is kept too long.
After you open it, keep it in a plastic bag

A package of floral clay

A small bottle of Elmer's glue (for repairs)

A piece of Styrofoam. This is optional, but handy to have on hand to stick your flowers in as you wire them for your arrangements

Sand

When I first started drying flowers, I tried a number of different drying agents, alone or in combination. Except for its weight, a problem I will show you how to overcome, I found sand to be by far the easiest, cheapest, pleasantest, cleanest, and most all-around satisfactory material. Borax and sand burned flowers left in the mixture too long. Cornmeal and sand attracted bugs. Fuller's earth left a residue. Silica gel dried flowers quickly but overdried them if the timing was not calculated precisely, which was difficult to do (and besides, I don't like to baby-sit my flowers). Silica gel is also quite expensive, and even though it can be dried out in the oven and re-used, one would have to buy quite a lot to start with in order to dry more than just a few flowers at a time. For my purpose, which is to dry flowers simply for fun, I have found sand to be a perfectly satisfactory drying agent, without the problems I have encountered with other materials.

While any *dry* sand will dry flowers, the results will

vary with the quality of the sand. In an emergency, I have even dried flowers with Michigan road sand, but I don't recommend that you use it.

The sand that will give you the best results, and the pleasantest one to use, is silica sand, also known as "glass sand." It is pure white and looks and feels like sugar. I buy it in bulk from builders' supply companies for a few cents a pound. Look in the yellow pages of your phone book under "sand" or check the sources at the end of this chapter.

You may find this pure white sand at some nurseries, and it is also available at Woolworth and Woolco stores, where a two-pound bag, at this writing, costs less than thirty cents. I'd suggest starting out with at least ten pounds, preferably twenty. In some parts of the country, this floral sand may be yellow, not white, but, as you will see, it works just as well.

The silica sand, or floral sand, is such a joy to work with that eventually, I suspect, you will want to use it exclusively, even if you have to go to some trouble to find it. Meanwhile there are other kinds of sand, mostly free, that will work very well.

Fine white beach sand is a silica sand though it needs to have the impurities and the salt removed. To use beach sand, put it in a pail, fill the pail with water, stir up the sand, and let it settle. Pour off the excess water. Do this two or three times until the water is clean. Although the sand remaining in the pail will eventually dry, you can speed the process considerably by dividing the sand up into flat baking dishes or pie plates and placing it in the sun. If you are really in a hurry, just put the plates in a warm oven. Do be sure the sand is perfectly dry before using it, though. Since you can re-use the same sand almost indefinitely, this isn't as much trouble as it sounds.

Don't use beach sand that is full of ground-up pebbles and shells. Even though you can remove the salt and get it clean, the particles that remain will be too large and uneven.

White or yellow dune sand and the sand from lake or river bottoms is also good. Wash any of this sand in the same way you would ocean beach sand. Although it may not be salty, it really isn't clean enough for best results unless it is washed. Dune sand, particularly, may need several stirrings and settlings; there is more dirt in those white dunes than you think!

Masonry sand — the yellow sand known to gardeners as "sharp" builders' sand — is not satisfactory. It has too much clay in it. Even if you were to wash out all the clay, the remaining particles would be too large. In some parts of the country, masonry sand is gray. Gray sand fades the color out of your flowers.

Most outdoor sandbox sand, whether gray or yellow, is unsuitable for the same reasons that masonry sand is. In some places, though, sandbox sand is ocean beach sand, and can be treated as described above.

In other words, what you want is clean white or yellow sand with uniform small particles.

Since sand is heavy, you cannot simply dump it over your flowers, or you'll end up with pressed flowers rather than natural, three-dimensional ones. The way you overcome this problem is simply by pouring the sand *gently* under, around, and over the flowers, and using your fingers or the wrong end of your paintbrush to hold the petals and leaves in their natural shape. It isn't difficult, but it is important, which is why you will find me constantly reminding you to be gentle.

The other trick is to avoid using too much sand. You need only cover the flowers, not bury them deeply. And, finally, when it comes time to pour off the sand, once again the answer is to be slow and gentle so that the weight of the sand doesn't pull the flowers with it.

Because the sand-drying process seems so simple, beginners sometimes tend to ignore these instructions. Although I can understand your impatience to dry a lot of flowers in a hurry and uncover them quickly to see what they look like, it takes only a very few minutes more to do it correctly, and the results will merit that little bit of extra care.

Sources for Sand

Frank's Nursery Sales, Inc. 6399 E. Nevada, Detroit, Michigan 48234. Through its own stores in Michigan, Ohio, Illinois, Indiana, and Minnesota, sells silica sand in twenty-pound bags. Also a fine white sand (suggested for patio outdoor ashtrays) in smaller bags.

The Smith Chemical and Color Company, 104 Dunkirk Street, Jamaica, Long Island, New York 11201. Supplies silica sand to retail outlets.

Whitehead Brothers Company, 6060 Hanover Road, Florham Park, New Jersey 07932. Supplies both silica sand and Cape Cod beach sand to retail outlets. The same company has a branch office at 17 Exchange Place, Providence, Rhode Island 02903.

Lane Mountain Silica Company, Valley, Washington 99181. Supplies silica sand to both wholesale and retail outlets on the West Coast.

F. W. Woolworth and Woolco stores. White or yellow floral sand, under various trade names, including Flora Sand, available in two-pound bags.

2. Sand-Drying Techniques

Materials

Boxes	Florist's wire
A bucket of sand	Scissors
Paper cups	Wire clippers

A piece of shirt cardboard, or any lightweight cardboard

TRY TO FIND a place in your house where you won't have to pick up and put away your materials each time you work at your project; while this isn't essential, it's certainly a help. A card table is big enough. Store your boxes under the table. You can put your bucket of sand on the floor at your side or on the table. It's a good idea to keep your tools in a small open box (and to remember to put them back when you are finished).

For your first attempt, I would suggest that you try one flower or two of a kind, such as two medium-sized zinnias or medium-sized daisies. I have found that most people, in their anxiety to create a dried bouquet, try to do too many flowers at a time, with the result that they lose patience and become careless.

Just one more preliminary word before we begin. Throughout this book, you will notice that I dry some flowers with their own stems and leaves, and others by replacing the natural stems with wire. In many cases this is simply a matter of choice — wired flowers can be bent into more graceful forms in an arrangement; natural stems, though remaining stiff, may retain their foliage — but sometimes it is a question of what will or will not work. You couldn't very well strip off each blossom from a tall delphinium spire, for instance, and then wire each bell back onto an artificial stem. (Or if you could, you wouldn't want to!) Another factor that enters into the decision is whether the foliage is worth trying to save; it very often isn't.

For my first flower, I have chosen a medium-sized zinnia in one of the lighter pastel shades. Although zinnias may be dried with their own stems and leaves, I prefer to use wire so that I can bend the stem however I like when I make the arrangement. Zinnias are sturdy and dry very well, but if you don't have any, look in your garden or florist shop for a flower of similar conformation — or simply read this section through and then move on to the instructions for daisy-type flowers.

Leave a few inches of the natural stem on the zinnia. Insert a piece of medium-heavy florist's wire (number 18) through the center of the blossom, pushing it about halfway down through the stem.

Cut wire flush at the blossom end with your clippers. Three or four inches of wire is enough to leave for stem — later you will add to the wire stem. After the zinnia has dried, you will find that it is firmly attached to the wire. If your flower's head is less solid than a zinnia's, bend the end of the wire into a hook and push it into the center of the blossom, out of sight.

Pour an inch or so of sand into a small shoe box. For this, your first attempt, dry only one zinnia in the box. With experience, you may be able to put more than one flower in a box of this size.

To make the support for the flower head, take a piece of cardboard — approximately three by five inches — and fold it in half, lengthwise. Cut a notch in the fold.

3

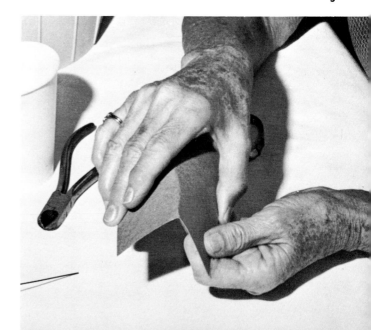

1

2

4 5

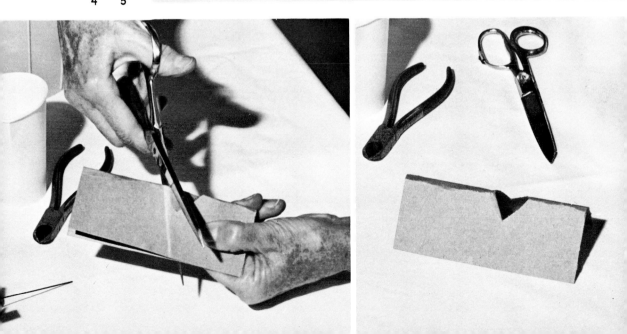

Put the notched support in your drying box and rest the flower head on the notch. You want to be sure that the flower is high enough in the box so that the bottom petals aren't crushed or bent, yet low enough so that the entire flower can be covered by sand. For this reason, a shallow box would not do for a flower of this size.

Crease a paper cup to make a pouring spout, and fill the cup with sand. Now comes the only tricky part. Since sand is heavy, if you simply poured it over the flower the weight would press it out of shape. To preserve the flower in its natural form takes two hands and a light touch. Use your fingers to separate the petals as you sift the sand slowly into, under, and all around the flower. Cover the blossom completely, but just until it is out of sight.

Be sure to label your box with the name of the flower and the date it was put in to dry. A three-by-five card

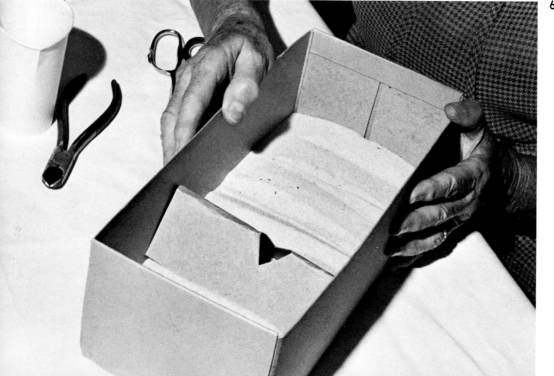

6

is handy because you can make notes on the results of your experiment and file them for future use. (For example, you might jot down the color of the flower before and after it was dried, as well as the length of time it took to dry.)

Don't cover the box. Do, however, place the cover under the box, since later you may want to use the covered box to keep your dried flowers until you are ready to use them.

Store the drying box in any *dry* place in your house where it can remain undisturbed. The drying time for flowers ranges from one to three weeks, depending on the thickness of the various parts of the flower, the water content, and the amount of humidity in the place where you are storing them. A damp cellar is obviously unsuitable but almost any other place is all right. Instructions for testing and uncovering dried material will be found in the next chapter.

"Flat" flowers, like daisies, coreopsis, gaillardia, painted daisies, black-eyed Susans and similar daisy-types, dry in a more natural position if they are placed in the drying medium face up. As a rule, short-petaled blossoms hold up much better than the long-petaled ones.

Leave about an inch or two of the natural stem on these daisy-like flowers and insert about four inches of wire through the face and stem of the flower, following the instructions for the zinnia.

10

11

Bend the wire at right angles, so that you can get several flowers in one box. Put an inch or so of sand in the bottom of the drying box and place the flowers on the sand, face up.

With the "wrong" end of your paintbrush, lift the petals so that you can pour the sand under, between, and over them to achieve a natural, rather than a pressed-flower, look.

12

Flowering branches, such as forsythia, dogwood, and crab apple, and tall-spired flowers — delphinium, lark-spur, lupine, etc. — will be dried on their own stems or branches. Use a long box and the notched-tent support. Make a notch for each stalk.

Place the branch or stalk on the notched support, and hold it lightly with one hand while you pour sand under and on the branch, until it is just covered. Spire flowers and branches usually take two or three weeks to dry because of the stems.

14

Little flowers with bunchy heads, like ageratum, should be dried in an upright position. Leave the natural stems and leaves on the flowers. Some of the leaves may not dry well; ageratum leaves, though fragile, retain their green color very well.

To dry small, "single-headed" flowers, such as roses, rosebuds, little zinnias, and marigolds, leave about one and a half inches of the natural stem. Make a hook at one end of a piece of four-inch wire, and insert the wire through the flower head, as described in the directions for the zinnia. Be sure to push the hook out of sight. Bend the wire stem up sharply.

Put about two to three inches of sand in the bottom of a paper cup or cottage cheese carton, and stick the flower into this.

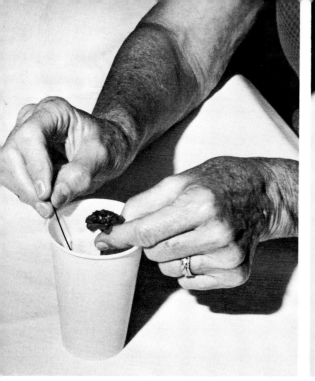 

Pour the sand very gently around the flower, controlling the contour of the petals with your other hand or the wrong end of a paintbrush. Be sure to let the petals separate a little, with the sand sifted among them. Your flower will dry faster and look more natural. Most flowers dried in this way will take one to two weeks.

Green foliage dried in sand will keep its shape and color better than when it is dried in air. Since good foliage subjects for drying are harder to find than are flowers, use the sand method whenever you can. Leather-leaf fern from the florist is one of the few ferns that dry extremely well.

Some leaves dry well but do not remain firmly attached to their branches after they have dried. And sometimes, even though they remain attached, you may

17

want to forgo the stiff natural branch for the flexibility that you can achieve with a wired one. This is particularly true in the case of vines. Large ivy leaves are easy to do. Dry the leaves separately, without attaching any wire.

After the leaves are dried, make a "vine" out of wire and attach the leaves to the artificial vine with florist's tape. What you see below is a box of dried ivy leaves and a finished branch.

18

3. Uncovering Sand-Dried Materials

ONE OF THE ADVANTAGES that sand has over other drying agents is that you cannot hurt a flower by leaving it in the sand too long. In general, one to three weeks is a fair estimate of the sand-drying period. Under the comments on specific flowers and greens that I have dried, you will find estimates as to drying time. It is difficult to give these with exactitude, since size, atmospheric conditions, and individual differences among even the same kinds of flowers affect them greatly. Fortunately, you can test for dryness and then, if more time is needed, simply recover the exposed test petals or leaves with more sand and put the box away for a few more days.

To test, gently pour off a little sand until you uncover a petal or leaf, as well as the stem if you are drying that too. Remember that each of these may have a different drying time, so be sure you test all parts of the specimen. A perfectly dried flower will feel like paper. It will also

19

20

be very fragile now, so everything you do from this point on must be done even more gently!

Though your sand can be reused indefinitely, you'll have to sift it occasionally to remove the debris of shattered petals and leaves — have your supply bucket or bowl handy when you are ready to start uncovering your flowers.

To pour off the sand, point one corner of the drying box toward your container and let the sand sift off slowly until almost all of the sand has been removed. Your flower will stay in place fairly well up until this point.

Keep the box corner pointed toward the receiving container and continue pouring off the sand as you very gently remove the flower from the box. If you have dried more than one flower in a box, remove the one nearest you first, working down as the sand sifts off.

Although it isn't essential, it's handy to have a block of Styrofoam to stick your flowers in, especially if you are working with more than one at a time. In any event, remember that your dried flowers are fragile, without the resiliency that they had when they were fresh.

With your artist's paintbrush, carefully brush away any grains of sand that may cling to the petals or leaves. Once again — at the risk of being repetitious — I must remind you of the need to be gentle. It is better to leave a little sand on the petals than to break them.

Unless you are planning to use it immediately, your dried material is now ready to be stored. Use a box of any appropriate size, and wad up facial tissues to support flower heads or other delicate parts that might be broken. Cover the box and label it with the name or names of the contents and the date. This will save you a lot of frustration and unnecessary handling when you come to making the bouquet. Put the box in a dry closet, cupboard, drawer, or any *dry* place where it won't be in your way.

4. Air Drying

Materials

Metal coat hangers

Pipe cleaners   String

AIR DRYING, as a method of preserving flowers, seems almost too obvious to need explanation. Some flowers and foliage may be dried simply by putting them in a vase without water, without any previous preparation at all. This works well for small and medium-sized pussy willow branches, eucalyptus leaves, wild grasses, and sea lavender, among others.

Most of your air-dried flowers, though, should be hung upside down in a dry dark place. A closet or attic is fine, but avoid damp cellars and garages. To hang your plant material, wind a pipe cleaner *tightly* around three or four stems of the flowers or foliage. It is important to bind the stems tightly because they will shrink

21

as they dry and may fall. Tie a piece of string to the other end of the pipe cleaner, and then tie the string to a coat hanger. By using string of varying lengths, you can make good use of your space without crowding and still allow good air circulation around your drying materials.

You could, of course, skip the pipe cleaners and simply tie the stems with the string. The advantage of the pipe cleaners is that they allow you to remove one or two stems at a time and then to rewind the other stems tightly, to remain hanging until you are ready to use them.

In general, air-dried material is used as fillers in your arrangements. It adds both softness and an airy outline, and gives the bouquet a finished look.

Good candidates for air drying include the "everlastings," baby's breath, goldenrod, yarrow, artemisia, and hydrangea. You'll find others listed in the chapters on flowers and greenery, but please don't restrict yourself to the flowers with which I've had experience. *Do* experiment with anything that takes your fancy; the worst that can happen is that you have to sweep some desiccated flowers off the floor.

Occasionally, you will find that flowers or foliage can be dried either in sand or in air. In these instances, you will almost always find that the sand method produces better results. However, it isn't always practical — it would take an awfully large bucket of sand to dry a bunch of baby's breath, which will serve its purpose as

filler just as well when dried by air. Coralbells do retain their color and shape better in sand, but maneuver-
ing sand into and around the tiny flowers may be difficult for a beginner; again, air drying is a good substitute.
Green foliage, on the other hand, is often much greener
in color and holds its shape so much better when done
in sand that here the extra effort is well worth the
trouble.

5. Making the Arrangement

I HOPE by this time you have had more successes than failures and that each success has given you such pleasure that you have forgotten about the flowers that didn't do too well.

In this chapter we will go through the procedures of arranging the materials shown in the step-by-step drying guides. Before you begin, set yourself up at a card table or any place where you'll have room to lay out all the materials conveniently.

Materials

Container: Choose a plain, medium-wide-mouthed vase. It is hard to work with a container with a very small opening. The vase should be ceramic, wood, or metal, but not clear glass. The vase will be filled with sand and it doesn't seem quite right not to be able to see the flower stems in a clear vase. Even if you were to forgo the sand, the dried and wired stems wouldn't look attractive anyway.

Florist's wire	Wire clippers
Florist's tape	Paintbrush
Floral clay	Bucket of sand
Scissors	Paper cup

Styrofoam block or another small bucket of sand

Before we start our arrangements, we must groom the flowers. This means straightening any bent wire stems, covering the wire with florist's tape, and lengthening any wire stems that are too short. If you select your container before you start, you will have an idea of how long you want the stems to be. If you find you have made them too long, you can cut them later with your wire clippers.

Cut the end of the florist's tape as shown. The angle cut makes it easier to wrap it neatly at the beginning and end.

Place the angle end of the tape vertically against the head of the flower and wrap in a spiral downward, stretching the tape somewhat as you go to make the covering on the wire tight. Don't cut more tape than you can handle easily, since you can always add more.

The pictures opposite show how to splice two wires

together. The same overlapping process is used to add a piece of wire to a natural stem.

Continue your spiral wrapping downward to the place where you will add another piece of wire to lengthen the stem. (To add extra height or flexibility to the natural stems of air-dried material or flowers that you have dried in sand on their natural stems, you may also want to use wire. In these cases, strip off the bottom flowerets or leaves if necessary and use an appropriately heavy wire, splicing as illustrated below.)

After the wire stems have been added, take your paintbrush and clean off any residue of sand from the flower heads. If it doesn't seem to want to come loose, leave

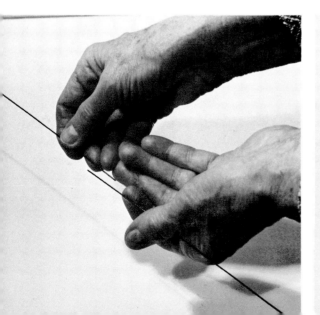 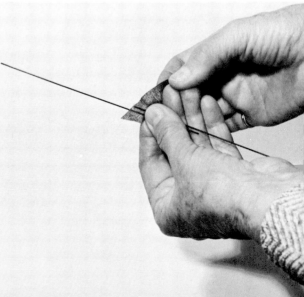

it. It probably won't show anyway and forcing it may shatter the flower.

It is a good idea to groom and stem as many of your flowers as you can before you start to make your bouquet. This will give you a visual picture of how the flowers will look and some idea of the space they will take in the container before you actually insert them in the vase. Naturally, if you need more, you can always groom more later.

As you stem each wired flower, stand it up in a bucket of sand or a piece of Styrofoam to keep it safe until it is ready to use.

Flowers, foliage, and filler material may be removed or changed to another place in your arrangement, but it is tricky to do because the other parts of the bouquet usually are pulled out with the change and some breakage may occur.

To prepare your vase, fill it with sand.

If you dampen the top two or three inches of sand

26

27   28

in the vase by trickling a little water over it, you will find that it is easier to keep the flowers in position as you are arranging them. Also, the sand hardens somewhat as it dries, which helps to keep the flowers in place. Remember, don't soak the sand; you only want it wet to about a finger's depth.

To make the flower holder even stronger, wet the sand, as described above, and then add a flattened piece of florist's clay — one half to three quarters of an inch thick — pinching it to the edge of the container to hold it in place.

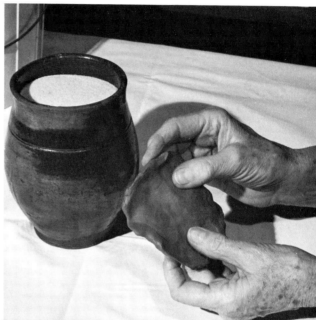

29   30

31

32

Start your arrangement by placing some of the tallest spire flowers at attractive angles, and then fill in with greenery and long-stemmed filler material.

With the framework of the design in place, add heavier light-colored spikes of flowers and more of the air-dried filler.

The long-stemmed "single-headed" flowers — zinnias, marigolds, and globe amaranths in the photograph — are arranged next. Use the lighter shades in this part of the bouquet.

As you work down toward the vase, adding your shorter-stemmed flowers, try also to include the deep-toned ones. Note that one flower head is bent over the

33

edge of the vase to give the arrangement a more interesting, graceful line.

Finish up with the flowers that have the deepest color. This keeps the arrangement from looking top-heavy. Be sure to include the small as well as the large. Now stand back and look over your arrangement. For balance, fullness, and contrast, tuck in pieces of light filler material wherever you think it is needed. The pieces will stay in place without long stems, so don't disrupt the arrangement by trying to anchor them into the base.

It is difficult to make any major changes in a dried

arrangement, particularly one of this kind. However, if time, childish hands, or pouncing kittens play havoc with a few flowers or fillers, you can generally replace them.

It is also possible — although I don't recommend it for beginners — to move an entire arrangement from one container to another. If you plan to do this, don't use the sand and floral-clay base in your vase. Instead, cut a one-and-one-half-to-two-inch piece of Styrofoam to fit the top of the container. Make sure that it fits snugly, or the arrangement will topple.

A real advantage of the Styrofoam base is that you

can remove an arrangement, intact, to store it over the summer. (Of course you *can* store an arrangement in the vase, but that takes up more room and leaves you one less vase for fresh flowers.)

Unlike house plants, dried arrangements thrive in dry, heated rooms and go limp when the humidity is high. In effect, this is perfect timing, for it means that just when the fresh flower season is over, you can start filling your home with your dried flower bouquets.

How long will a dried arrangement last? This is one of the questions I am most often asked, and one difficult to answer. As with the flowers themselves, there are simply too many factors involved to give any precise time limit. It depends in part on the flowers you use and in part on the place where you use them. A mixed arrangement may contain some short-lived flowers and some that could last as long as five years. If the whole arrangement begins to look shabby or fall apart, it is sometimes possible to save some of the material; just put it back in a storage box and use it again when you need it.

I have had an arrangement in the Toledo Museum of Art that has lasted as long as two years, but in a museum the temperature and humidity are controlled. Although I do most of my drying from spring to fall, when the flowers in my garden (and in the "wild") are in bloom, I store these in covered boxes in a dry closet or drawer and make the arrangements during the fall and winter months.

The greatest enemies of dried flower arrangements are people, cats, light, and moisture:

People just *have* to touch a bouquet to see if it is real — or to see how it feels. In the process, they break off petals and the tips of foliage.

Cats tend to pounce right into the arrangement. I think they imagine they see something moving among the flowers. If you have cats, I guess the only thing to do is to keep your arrangements in an inaccessible spot.

Light fades the flowers, sooner or later. Don't put your arrangement in direct sun or a bright light. It is also unwise to keep the arrangement directly under a table lamp, although, of course, you can move it there for special occasions.

Moisture is self-explanatory.

Part II

Flowers and Foliage

6. The Flowers

THE FLOWERS AND FOLIAGE in this chapter and the next are those that I have dried with the most consistent success and have found to be useful and attractive in arrangements. Please don't consider these as "lists" of all the materials you can dry but rather as notes from my own experience. It isn't possible to present instructions for drying flowers as one would a scientific formula — you could do exactly as I say and come out with a different result, perhaps better, perhaps worse. And so, next time, could I. For example, I've had the experience of drying two apparently identical blossoms from the same plant and had them come out different colors! The bracken fern I pick in the Middle West dries to shades of bronze or mustard, yet a friend on the East Coast tells me *her* bracken, which grows in sandy soil near the ocean, dries to a silvery green.

If you consider the number of variables involved — the kind of sand you use for drying, the soil and climate in which the flower grows, the temperature and humidity of your house, the condition and age of the flower when it goes into the drying box (to name only the most obvious ones)—you can understand why no two flowers will dry identically. For me, that's half the fun and half the challenge.

Still, a beginner would do well to pick the easiest and most reliable flowers to start with. You'll find a list of these at the end of this chapter, along with a list of flowers that dry well but have petals that droop. Once you become interested in this hobby, dry anything that strikes your fancy and appeals to you. You may have flowers I've never tried, or succeed where I have failed. Experimenting really is a good part of the fun!

Flowers

ACACIA. Buy it at the florist's and dry it in sand for a week or ten days. If you dry it in the air method, the small yellow balls will tend to shrink. In sand, though, they last several years.

AGERATUM. Sand-dry, seven to ten days. Dry small bunches of the flowerets, with two to three inches of their own stems. Stand the flowerets up in about an inch of sand in the drying box (Figure 14). Although the leaves of ageratum are fragile, they stay a good green, so I dry them on the stem with the flowers.

The blue ageratum keeps its color, but in my experience the pink reverts back to blue in the drying process.

Ageratum, pink rosebuds, and white baby's breath make a charming bouquet. Or place ageratum in a low bowl with two- or three-inch plumes of red celosia.

ARTEMISIA. Air-dry for one week. The light silver-gray foliage makes wonderful filler material in dried arrangements. The variety I grow is called Silver Frost.

BABY'S BREATH. Air-dry, five days to a week. Both the white and pink varieties are very useful for taking the heavy look away from bouquets.

BEE BALM. Also known as Oswego Tea. Dry the pink and light red shades in sand, from eight to ten days. Dry the flower head and stem intact, but remove the foliage as it is too fragile to use when it is dry. It takes a light hand to pour the sand around the delicate parts of this flower head. Use the notched cardboard support and gently pour the sand around and over the flower until it is *just covered* — too much weight could be disastrous. When you pour off the sand at the end of the drying period, go very slowly to avoid any separation of the flower parts.

BUTTERFLY WEED. Follow the directions for ageratum. Cut off the bunches of flowerets and dry them in sand for one week. Don't try to retain the leaves of the butterfly weed. After drying, you may make a longer stem by splicing a light wire (number 22) to the original stem.

Although the flowerets shrink quite a bit, the orange color is so unusual that the butterfly weed adds a lot to an arrangement.

CARNATIONS. The carnations you buy at the florist's dry well. Dry them in sand following the basic instructions for small single-headed flowers.

When dried, this flower head will need extra support to keep the petals from falling out of their natural "holder." You can accomplish this by wrapping your florist's tape tightly around the green base of the flower before you continue taping down the wire stem.

Small corsages of carnations dry well. Simply remove the ribbon, place the whole corsage in the box, and sift sand under, around, and over the entire corsage. The length of drying time will depend on the size of the corsage, of course. To preserve it, see Chapter 9.

CELOSIA. Air-dry about two weeks, depending primarily on the thickness of the stalk. Remove the foliage.

CLEMATIS. Sand-dry, two to three weeks. Dry six- to eight-inch sections of the vine, leaving both the flowers and foliage intact. Place the vine on a half-inch of sand, letting it lie naturally, with the flower face up. Carefully pour the sand over and around it without disturbing the position of any part of the flower, leaves, or vine. About three sprays, of varying lengths, dried in three separate boxes, will be enough to make a charming arrangement in a low bowl.

I'm sorry to say that the petals will probably droop in about three or four months, but the vine is so beautiful that it is well worth the effort.

My experience has only been with white clematis from a vine that has lost its identity as to variety. The white stayed a pure white — unusual for dried white flowers of any kind. I would not hesitate to dry all colors of clematis.

COCKSCOMB. Pick the cockscomb to dry before it starts to go to seed, and follow the instructions for celosia (to which it is related). If the cockscomb is large, it may be cut apart with a scissors *after drying.* Splice wire to the dried stems. Split cockscomb are very effective in a mass bouquet.

CORALBELLS. Dry in sand or air for one week. Until you become experienced, you are probably better off using the air method — the bells are so tiny that it is hard to avoid flattening them when you pour sand over them. However, when you feel you have a light enough touch, do try the sand method as the results are lovely. Both the coral and red shades of this flower retain their color well. Use them with other flowers as they are too delicate-looking by themselves.

DAFFODILS. This is a hard one so don't attempt it until you have considerable experience and quite a bit of patience.

Cut the natural stem about an inch and a half from the flower base. Push a four-inch piece of wire *horizontally* halfway through the green base of the flower, then bend both ends of wire down to form a loop securing the flower. Later, of course, you will add to the wire stem, but meanwhile this arrangement will make it possible for you to place the flower head, cup up, in a small box or cottage cheese container. Dry one daffodil to a container.

With the cup facing up, pour sand first around the petals of the flower, just enough to cover them. Then fill the flower cup with sand. Last of all, pour sand around the outside of the flower cup until all parts are covered.

Daffodils take a week to ten days to dry. Be very, very careful when you pour the sand off — the flower is extremely fragile. Adjust the wire so the flower head is upright and stick it in a block of Styrofoam until you are ready to store or use the daffodil. If you are going to store it, put it in a box on an inch layer of sand, very much as you did at the start of the drying process. Don't crowd the box. Put a cover on it and try not to jar it at any time.

I've had better luck drying florists' daffodils than my own garden varieties. You can usually get them as early

as February, and for some reason they keep their clear color while garden ones sometimes discolor in the drying process.

DAHLIAS. Dry only the small ones and the pompons. Remove the foliage and dry the flowers in sand according to the basic instructions for drying daisies. Depending on size, they will take from ten days to two weeks to dry.

DAISIES. Sand-dry for one week to ten days according to basic instructions. (See figures 10, 11, 12.) Whether you buy daisies, grow them, or pick the wild ones, select flowers with short stubby petals, particularly those with petals that are wide at the base. Long slender petals tend to droop, and petals that are very narrow at the point where they are attached to the center of the flower are more likely to drop off. (If you've always thought that every daisy looks alike, you'll be surprised at the variety in conformation. Drying flowers teaches you to become extremely observant!)

DELPHINIUM. Dry in sand, two to three weeks. (See Figure 13.)

All colors dry well, with little change of color. This is a good source of white for bouquets. As you have gathered by now, white flowers that remain white are not easy to find.

When you manipulate the stalk of the delphinium, be

careful to lay it *lightly* on the cardboard support, so that sand can be sifted beneath the bottom blossoms; this will keep them from flattening out. Carefully fill the bottom air spaces first and then pour the sand around the rest of the flower, remembering not to distort the blossoms as you pour. The leaves may be left on or removed, as you prefer.

DIANTHUS. Dry these annual pinks in sand, for one or two weeks. Remove the foliage and cut the stem. Dry them on number 22 wire, following the directions for drying small, single-headed flowers. (See Figures 15 and 16.)

When it comes time to wrap the stem with floral tape, follow the instructions in this chapter for carnations. Dianthus are lovely alone or in a mixed bouquet.

DOGWOOD. Dry the branches in sand from two to three weeks, retaining the leaves. You can dry branches of any length, but I advise you to stick to a length of twelve inches or less. Three or five branches of different lengths look beautiful in a small bowl or slender-necked vase.

Follow the basic instructions for spire flowers (Figure 13) and give careful attention to each blossom to retain the original contour. To avoid making "flat" flowers, work sand into the air spaces beneath them. Do the same for the leaves. A flat lollipop stick is a useful tool for this purpose. To store the branches, lay them

on an inch of sand in the covered storage box. I sometimes add a bit of wadded facial tissue to support parts
of the blossoms.

GAILLARDIA. Dry in sand for two weeks according
to the instructions for daisies. The flower dries well,
but the mahogany center will turn reddish brown. Gaillardia is stunning in a mixed bouquet, although the long
petals will eventually droop.

GERANIUM. Dry in sand, on their own stems, for ten
days. Follow the instructions for drying zinnia, using
the notched cardboard support. Remove the leaves, since
they won't remain green. The flower heads are beautiful
in a mass bouquet.

GLOBE AMARANTH. Air-dry, ten days to two weeks.
Hang in small bunches, five or six stalks to a bunch, retaining the natural foliage. This is one of the most useful of the "everlastings."

The globe amaranths are usually light or dark purple.
I have also found them in white, pink, and yellow-orange.
The white turns a light cream in the drying process. The
yellow-orange turns to a straw color with a light orange
shading. The pink and the purples retain their original
color.

GOLDENROD. Dry in sand or air for about ten days.
Keep flowers on their natural stems, but don't retain the
foliage as it shatters easily. Goldenrod keeps its natural

form equally well in the sand or air method, but the color is better retained in the sand method.

Dry lots of goldenrod, since it makes wonderful background material. The goldenrod I dry is a cultivated variety known as Cloth of Gold, but the wild goldenrods — there are almost a hundred different species, most of them native to this continent! — are dried in the same way. Try the small ones in sand; it is probably more practical to dry the large-headed goldenrods by the air method. In any case, pick the flower before it is too full blown and beginning to go to seed.

(Goldenrod, by the way, is not the plant that gives people hay fever; it is the ragweed that ripens at the same time.)

HEATHER. Dries beautifully by the air method. I've only dried heather purchased at the florist's, but do try your own if you live where you can grow it in your garden.

HOLLYHOCKS. Dry the double hollyhocks in sand for about two weeks. (The single hollyhocks won't hold up long enough to make it worth the trouble.) Select only the light shades; the dark ones dry to an unattractive color.

Keep the small stem on the flower and proceed as follows:

Make a hook at the end of a four-inch piece of wire. Put the wire through the head, pushing it through so that the hook is buried in the center of the flower face. Bend the wire, as in the basic instructions for daisies, so that the flower may be dried face up.

At this point, the technique for drying hollyhocks differs somewhat from that of the other flowers we've discussed, so please read the directions carefully.

First, put an inch to an inch-and-a-half layer of sand in the bottom of the box. Next, make shallow depressions, one for each flower, in the sand. Don't attempt to do more than three flowers in a box as you will have difficulty pouring off the sand without damaging the dried flowers. Lay the flower heads in the depressions, face up. With the end of your paintbrush or a lollipop stick, separate the petals as you pour sand lightly between them. Use only a thin layer of sand between the petals. Finish by covering the entire flower head, using just enough sand to cover the flowers.

When you pour off the sand, shake the hollyhocks *gently* to remove the sand from between the petals. It won't all come out, but that doesn't matter since you won't see it anyway.

Hollyhocks may be used in a mixed bouquet, but too many of them will dwarf your other flowers, so be especially careful to watch the balance when you use them in an arrangement.

HYDRANGEA. Air-dry, one week to ten days. This is one flower I would advise you not to dry in sand. If you want to retain the leaves, dry the stalks singly and use the hydrangeas alone in a vase because the leaves become very fragile and will shatter if you try to incorporate them in a mixed bouquet.

If you strip the leaves, use the flower heads intact on their natural stems or break off the dried flowerets to fill in spots in an arrangement. If your bouquet is not going to be moved around, you can insert the flowerets into a partially finished arrangement without adding stems, since they will cling to parts of the other dried materials.

All varieties of hydrangeas dry well. When matured, the colors may be blue, pink, mauve, rose, beige-rose, or white. Sometimes the whites get brown spots when they are dried; you'll have to gamble on that. Be sure to cut some of the green flower heads to dry as they stay a good green and greatly enhance a bouquet.

LARKSPUR. This is an annual delphinium, and one of the most rewarding of all the flowers you can dry, so try to do a lot of them. Dry in sand for one week, following the directions for delphinium and spire flowers (Figure 13). The foliage is so fragile that it virtually disappears in the drying process and thus doesn't have to be removed before you put the larkspur in the sand.

A bouquet of larkspur, with a little greenery as background, makes a superb arrangement.

LIATRIS (Blazing Star). Dry in sand for two weeks. Dry shades of purple, lavender, and white for lovely additions to your dried flower supply. Follow the directions for spire flowers (Figure 13).

LUPINE. Sand-dry, two weeks. Remove the foliage. This is another spire flower that keeps its form well. The flower does fade some during the drying process, but the structure of the flower is so interesting in a bouquet that it is worth preserving. Try all colors.

LYTHRUM (Morden's Pink). Sand-dry for about a week, following the instructions for drying spire flowers. Take care not to let one side dry flat. These are lovely stalks of deep pink flowers that keep their color well.

MARIGOLDS. Sand-dry, one to three weeks, following the instructions for zinnias. The yellow and orange marigolds will retain both their form and color well. The maroon or mahogany markings on the two-toned varieties tend to turn brown.

I don't advise you to dry the large, heavy-headed marigolds. They are awkward to use and so dominate a mixed bouquet that one can't see the flowers for the marigolds! The small single marigolds, though, are excellent in arrangements. Dry these according to the instructions for daisies or small, single-headed flowers (Figures 15 and 16).

NARCISSUS. Dry all varieties of narcissus according to the directions for daffodils. Give them ten days in sand. Use them only when the house is very dry in the winter.

PANSIES. Dry in sand, ten days to two weeks. Leave as much of the natural stem as you can — sometimes a pansy has practically none — and insert a four- or five-inch piece of fine wire *up* through the hollow stem and through the hard little crooked base of the flower to the center of the face. Cut the wire flush with the face. Bend the wire and dry the pansies, face up in a bed of sand, according to the basic instructions for daisies. Don't do more than three or four pansies in one box. Fill the air spaces under the flower and, with the hard end of a paintbrush to help, pour some sand between the petals to retain the natural contours of the face.

Since the risk of breaking the dried flowers is great, don't try to wrap the wire stems with florist's tape. Use the flowers in a small vase or regular pansy holder in which only the faces show. With the wire stems, they can be bent at any angle you wish, but do be careful. Display the arrangement when the house is closed and heated, as pansies droop quickly in humidity. The light blues and yellows keep their colors well. Sometimes the purple is pleasing, sometimes it turns too dark. Try all colors.

PEONIES. Sand-dry, two to three weeks, on their own stems with the foliage left on according to the instructions for drying zinnias. A large shoe box will hold one peony head and foliage. Choose a small or medium-sized flower; the large ones are just too big to dry conveniently and the smaller blooms are equally effective in a vase. Dry extra foliage to fill in around the flowers.

PURPLE CONEFLOWER (Rudbeckia). Dry in sand, without foliage, one week to ten days, according to the basic instructions for drying zinnias.

Take careful note of the way the petals of this flower point downward and try to retain this characteristic as you dry the coneflower, or it will end up looking like a daisy.

In spite of the fact that the petals of the coneflower have a natural "droop," they stay crisp and do not go limp in an arrangement; obviously they have more substance to them than does the average long slender petal. I have had some that have kept their form for over two and a half years — they don't look any different than they did the day I took them out of the sand. My experience has been with a variety called "The King" with a maroon-red center and petals of rosy lavender. The petals turn lavender in the drying.

PUSSY WILLOW. Air-dry small and medium-size branches by standing them in a container. The very large ones should be hung, or the "pussies" will stick out awkwardly. I have used some branches for as long as five years in various arrangements.

QUEEN ANNE'S LACE (Wild Carrot). This lovely wildflower is found virtually everywhere and is one of the most important flowers you can find for dried arrangements, so pick a lot of it. It is not on any "protected" list of wildflowers.

To dry, leave the long stems on the plant and place the flower heads, *face down,* on a shallow bed of sand. Cover them gently with a light layer of sand, trying to get the sand around the tiny "snowflakes" of the flower head in such a way as not to flatten them. Let the stems fall any way they wish over the edge of the box, without covering them. When the stems and flowers are dry, the heads will be bent on the stems in such a way that they will be easy to use and at a graceful angle in your arrangements.

Although I have seen Queen Anne's lace colored in some bouquets, I think it strikes a jarring note, rather like putting lipstick on a beautiful little child. Please don't.

ROSES. Sweetheart roses take ten days to two weeks in sand. The others, two to three weeks, depending on size. Follow the instructions for small, single-headed flowers (Figures 15 and 16).

It is almost impossible to say which roses will dry best; two of the same kind may turn out quite differently, but when they turn out well they are so beautiful that it is well worth your time and effort to experiment with any roses. Try them in their various stages of flowering, too, since the effect of a full-blown rose is as lovely in its own way as an opening bud.

I find that pink roses are the best color to dry. Some

whites turn a pretty cream color. Some yellows keep their color well, as do the light red and tangerine shades. The dark reds turn an unattractive color.

SALVIA (BLUE). Air-dry without foliage for two weeks. This is one of your most valuable flowers for dried arrangements, so do lots of it.

SALVIA (RED). This is an entirely different flower from the blue salvia and requires a different treatment. Dry it in sand for ten days, following the directions for delphinium and other spire flowers (Figure 13). Remove the foliage. Red salvia doesn't take as long to dry as delphinium because the stem isn't as dense. The red salvia dries to a lovely light red.

SNAPDRAGON. Dry in sand for two weeks. This isn't an easy flower to do because of the thickness of the stalk. You might try the dwarf varieties, which have much more slender stems.

Follow the directions for spire flowers (Figure 13). Strip off the foliage and try to get as much sand into the little "snaps" as you can so that they won't flatten out in drying. Dry the light pink or the yellow snapdragons and some light bicolor ones.

VERBENA. Dry in sand for one week, following the instructions for ageratum (Figure 14), but remove the foliage. Splice fine wire stem to the natural stem after the flowers are dry.

All colors of verbena remain clear and vivid. This is a beautiful flower to dry.

YARROW. Air-dry a lot of this. The wild yarrow is most often bone-colored, although you may be lucky enough to find some of the rare pink variety. Cultivated yarrow comes in yellow or bone. This is a very useful plant for dried arrangements.

ZINNIA. Dry in sand, from one to three weeks, following the basic instructions. Try all colors and sizes, as zinnias are very lovely alone or in combination with other flowers. Even the large ones with the long petals hold up well.

All shades of pink, yellow, orange, and lavender keep their colors well. White often turns a light gray. Light red may or may not go to magenta. Some deep reds keep their original colors; others do not. The two-toned flowers are also tricky.

If you keep the foliage on, use the zinnias alone, since the foliage and stems will be too stiff to incorporate into a bouquet with other flowers.

Best Bets

Although these flowers will hold up and stay crisp and firm longer than most, I still advise that all dried flowers be kept in storage in a covered box or dry closet during the summer months. They really are more effective on display in the winter anyway.

ageratum	larkspur
artemisia	liatris
baby's breath	lupine
bee balm	marigolds
butterfly weed	peony
celosia	purple coneflower
cockscomb	Queen Anne's lace
dahlia	roses
delphinium	salvia (both the blue and the red)
globe amaranth	snapdragon
goldenrod	verbena
heather	yarrow
hydrangea	zinnia

The "Wilters"

These flowers won't stand up in any atmosphere that is at all humid. Use them only when the heat is turned on and be sure to store them in a covered box in a dry place during the rest of the year. Even at best, though, you'll find that the "wilters" are shorter-lived than the flowers on the best-bet list.

clematis	gaillardia
daffodils	hollyhocks
daisies	narcissus
dogwood	pansies
flowering branches	tulips
violets	

7. Foliage and "Greenery"

NATURE PROVES to us the importance of greenery as a background; arrangements containing leaves or other greens are more effective than those composed of flowers alone. While there is no special difficulty about drying this material, the problem is finding the leaves, vines, ferns, and flower foliage that keep their color — which is why I have put quotation marks around "greenery."

I am continually experimenting with greens, and hope you will too. In general, look for leaves that aren't fragile, that have some substance to them so they won't shatter in the drying process. Look, too, for leaves that have a firm attachment to their branches and aren't likely to fall off. (Large leaves, however, can sometimes be dried separately and later attached to artificial wire stems.)

Color is less predictable. The only thing to do is experiment. Keep in mind that greenery doesn't always have to be green to be attractive. Daffodil leaves dry yellow and aren't a bit pretty, but geranium leaves turn tan and can add an interesting note to a fall bouquet.

Sooner or later, almost all foliage will fade. If it does, it can sometimes be replaced. Or the flowers can be saved and stored for another winter.

Look for greens any place and at any time. The ivy pictured in Chapter 2 was picked one day in January, from under a snow-covered bed of leaves. The parsley described in Chapter 11 was bought at a supermarket, also in winter. In some of my flower-drying experiments, the flowers were a failure, but the foliage was a success.

With the reminder that what follows is not a definitive list, but rather notes from my own experience, here are some good (and bad) candidates for foliage for dried arrangements:

Ferns

By far the best fern to dry is the LEATHERLEAF FERN, which you can buy at the florist's. Dry it in sand for one week. It keeps both its form and color very well.

Of the wild ferns I have tried, only the MAIDEN-HAIR FERN dries well and keeps its color. Dry it in sand for one week. BRACKEN, the common roadside fern, also dries well, but in my experience turns bronze or mustard color. It is attractive in fall bouquets. Dry

it in sand for ten days. Most of the other wild ferns are so fragile they simply shatter. If I lived in the Northeast, or other parts of the country where it grows, I would certainly try to dry the evergreen CHRISTMAS FERN, which has the same substance and deep color as the LEATHERLEAF FERN.

One kind of greenery that can sometimes be bought at the florist's is the EMERALD (or JADE) COMMODOR PALM. Take off a few of the stiff "leaves" and dry them singly, or dry the whole branch.

Shrubs and Vines

BOXWOOD. May be air-dried, but the results are much better in sand. Dry for a week to ten days, depending on the size of the bunches. Lay the small branches lightly on a base of sand in the drying box. Fill the air spaces around and under the tiny leaves and continue pouring the sand until the entire branch is covered. When the branches are dried, you can use them as they are or add a wire stem.

COTONEASTER. Dry branches eighteen inches or less in length in a bed of sand for a week to ten days. If you cut the branches just as the tiny pink flower is about to open, both the flower *and* the leaves will dry well.

HONEYSUCKLE. Although some people deplore the fact that the evergreen Japanese honeysuckle is so invasive that it takes over an area, crowding out more valuable wild plants, the honeysuckle vine is a marvelous gift to flower dryers. Its bright color and the interesting lines of its tendrils give a wonderful softening effect to dried arrangements, which often tend to be overly stiff. Dry lots of it; it is infinitely useful.

Dry sections of the vine, eighteen inches or less, on a thin layer of sand for one week. Be sure to let the vine lie naturally, and pour the sand under and around the leaves to preserve the contours. Pour the sand off very gently as the vine will be quite crisp when it is dry. Store it carefully, for the same reason.

IVY. Dry various lengths of this vine in sand. There are so many varieties of English ivy that it is impossible to give you a drying time. The large-leaved variety (Figure 18) took about a week to dry. You can dry the vines with the leaves attached or, as in the photograph, dry the leaves and then make an artificial wire vine; in some cases, the artificial vine will be more graceful than the real one. Use number 20 wire. Study the way the leaves are attached to the vine and try to copy the position and spacing as well as you can.

Sprays of ivy are attractive alone or with just a few flowers as a focal point with the ivy sprays branching out. Ivy is also useful as a background in a full bouquet of dried flowers.

LEMON LEAVES, purchased from the florist, may be dried on their branches in sand, for one week. The leaves turn light silver-green and hold their color indefinitely.

Flower Foliage and Green Plants

CLOVER. Pick the large, long-stemmed clover leaves for best results. These are the ones you find in fields, not your lawn. Dry them in sand, for one week. The green color is lovely, but the leaves are fragile, so handle them carefully. They are effective in small arrangements.

COLUMBINE. Dry the foliage in sand for five days. Lay it on a bed of sand and cover it lightly. It keeps its color well.

MINT. Dry the stalks in sand for ten days, following the directions for spire flowers. The mint leaves stay very green.

PARSLEY. Dry the curly variety in sand for one week. Dry large stems according to the directions for spire flowers. Small single stems may be placed upright in a bed of sand. Pour the sand around each stem evenly until all are covered at the same time. Parsley will keep its color for six to eight months.

ROSE FOLIAGE. Dry in sand for one week. The leaves stay a very good green and can be used in arrangements even if the flowers are not included.

VIOLET LEAVES. Dry in sand, four days to a week. They retain their good color for a long time.

8. Wildflowers

SO FAR AS basic techniques go, there is no difference between drying wild and cultivated flowers. Some of the flowers, vines, and greens described in the last two chapters are wild plants.

However, there are some generalizations that can be made about wildflowers.

Most of the early spring wildlings — like their garden counterparts — have a very high water content and do not dry well. Among these are the marsh marigolds, wild iris, and buttercups.

Many of the most appealing wildflowers are extremely delicate, particularly the spring woodland flowers. Although some of these can be dried, they require a much lighter touch than the garden species or hybrids. The more you handle flowers, the easier it will be for you to manage the delicate blossoms. Somehow one learns just the right touch, and it really doesn't take too long or too many disasters to learn.

On the other hand, the summer and fall field or road-side flowers or "weeds" — depending on your point of view — are generally very hardy, plentiful, beautiful in dried arrangements, and easy to handle. And last, but by no means least, they are neither rare nor endangered, and perfectly all right to pick. In this regard, I must caution you to be very sure that the wildflowers you gather are not on the list of protected plants in your area. Your local garden club or conservation society will be able to advise you about these. Or consult a book on wildflowers. While you may think that picking a flower, as opposed to digging one up, is harmless, there are certain plants, like the lady slipper, that die if the flower is picked. And of course if you pick a flower, you prevent it from going to seed and reproducing in that manner. In any event, don't ever denude an area of any wild plant.

In spring there is a great temptation to dry the first violet, and happily this is one spring flower that does dry well, and is perfectly all right to pick (so long as you stick to the "common" blue variety). There is also no better way to keep spring in our thoughts the rest of the year.

Violets have such delicate stems that it is virtually impossible to replace them with wire. Therefore, lay the flowers on a shallow bed of sand with their stems on and faces up. Gently sift the sand around them until they are just covered. Let them dry for about ten days.

Be very, very careful in removing sand from violets.

At the same time, pick a lot of violet leaves to dry. Lay these on a shallow bed of sand and sift the sand around and under the leaves, so that you preserve the contours and don't flatten them out. They will dry in about the same length of time as the flowers, and stay a good shade of green.

To arrange the bouquet of violets, ignore the instructions I've given you previously and make the bouquet in your hand *before* you put it in the vase. Choose a small container whose depth is about equal to the length of the violet stems. Milk glass is a pleasing background; you can find small vases in any variety store.

Take the violets, one at a time, into your hand to make a solid nucleus of violets with their faces up. Hold them carefully while you take some violet leaves and form a double circle around the flowers to make a lovely little nosegay. If you need a fuller bunch to fit into your vase, add more leaves. Now, with the bouquet still in your hand, trim all the stems evenly to the length that will make your bouquet flush with the edge of the container, and put them into the bowl. Sometimes, I put a little rosebud into the center of the arrangement. If you do this, be sure the rose is on a wire stem.

Try using other small flowers to make "in hand" bouquets after you practice a bit.

Another spring flower that dries quite well in spite of its delicacy is the wild columbine. Dry this with foliage, stem, and flower heads intact. Use the notched cardboard support, and dry only one stem of flowers to a box or you'll be in trouble when it comes time to pour off the sand. If some of the flower heads do come off, use a drop of glue applied with a toothpick to make the repair.

Dry the columbine for at least ten days. The flowers are equally lovely alone or in mixed arrangements.

In northern Michigan, where we spend most of our summers, I have found bunchberry growing along a trout stream. The flower of this wild ground cover resembles a dogwood blossom (it is in the same botanical family as the dogwood tree), with a cluster of small yellowish flowers surrounded by four large green-white bracts.

Bunchberry dries well for me. I do it with the leaves on, using the paper cup method. Place each flower, with leaves attached, in an upright position in the cup. Sift the sand gently around, making sure to retain the natural contours. Bunchberry needs about ten days to dry. Since it has a short stem, put it in a small vase or a low bowl. Just a few of these charming flowers make a lovely bouquet. Bunchberry is a protected plant everywhere, but picking it doesn't hurt the plant; just don't take more than a few.

The wild asters that grow in all parts of the country from late summer until almost the first snow are good flowers with which to experiment. They range in color from purple through all the lavenders down to white. The tiny white ones dry to an airy quality (similar to baby's breath) and are charming in combination with other flowers. Dry all of the asters in sand, on their own stems with the leaves on.

The common milkweed, in the same family as the butterfly weed, is not as spectacular as that orange relative, but an interesting flower to dry. Pick the lavender flower heads just before they are ready to burst into full bloom. Air-dry, with flower heads down, for two weeks or longer. (Butterfly weed is dried in sand; see directions in Chapter 6.)

Black-eyed Susans dry well, but don't hold up very long because the long slender petals tend to droop. This is equally true of the long-petaled wild daisies, as noted in the chapter on flowers.

Each year when I am in the country, I try to experiment with different wildflowers. I pick a bouquet of various flowers to see which dry well, and how well they hold up in arrangements.

Part III
Special Projects

9. The Memory Lingers On

DRIED FLOWERS are a lovely way to preserve the memory of special occasions. I somehow get a real thrill out of trying to create a permanent keepsake from a bride's bouquet, a groom's lapel flower, and any other flowers that are brought to me from a wedding or a reception. I must warn you, though, that a bridal bouquet will surely be in the poorest condition of any flowers you attempt to dry. After having been out of water for a long time, then held onto for dear life, crushed, and finally tossed, it presents a real challenge. That's part of the fun, but do be sure that the bride doesn't have any illusion that her keepsake will be a miraculous duplication of the original, fresh bouquet. Indeed, this may be one of those experiments that doesn't work out, but even then, as you'll see, all isn't lost. Besides, through the eyes of one to whom the flowers represent a sentimental occasion, anything you produce will look perfect.

Before you dry a bridal bouquet, make a rough sketch

or diagram of it. Next, take it apart carefully, observing how it was made. You might make a few notes for later reference. Put the ribbon, wires, pin, and any other artificial parts in a box and set them aside. When you come to reconstructing the bouquet, these will be invaluable.

If the stems are long enough, put the flowers and greenery in cool — not cold — water in a cool location and let them revive overnight. Be sure not to get water on the flower heads or the leafy parts of the greenery. When you remove them from the water the next day, pat each one dry with a piece of facial tissue before you start the drying process. Check the instructions in this book to find out which drying method is appropriate for each kind of flower. Where you have a choice between sand or air, always choose sand; these flowers will need all the help they can get.

After the drying period is complete, select the flowers that look the best and reconstruct your bouquet, necessarily in a smaller version. Besides being necessary, a small version is more practical for keeping anyway.

To store and display the keepsake flowers, get a clear plastic box from your florist, or any box with a clear plastic lid. Anchor the bouquet to the inside of the bottom of the box with Elmer's glue. When it has dried, put the lid on the box and seal it with transparent tape. Now take a piece of one-inch velvet ribbon, preferably white, green, or gold. Start at the center of the top or the bottom of the box and cover the tape with the ribbon, using a little glue to keep it in position. Last of all, make a flat tailored bow of the ribbon and glue it in place where the two ends of the ribbon meet. You now have a dust-proof, moisture-proof storage box that permits you to see the arrangement.

Frequently a bride will have a cymbidium orchid corsage to wear on her honeymoon trip. If she is careful with it, so the flower is not crushed or broken — and it is a short honeymoon — she may bring the corsage to you for preservation. Be sure to explain that while the orchid will retain its form, it will turn a nut brown.

Don't put the orchid in water, but proceed immediately to dry it by laying the flower on the sand and carefully filling in and around it with sand poured from a paper cup. Be sure to allow two weeks, at the very least, for an orchid to dry, as the water content in these flowers is quite high.

Small stationery boxes with clear plastic lids make excellent storage cases for corsages or little arrangements. To display an orchid, I glue a piece of mustard- or gold-colored velvet to the inside bottom of the box and then glue the corsage to this backing. If the flower is a memento from a wedding, I usually buy a ten-cent gold band, through which I loop the ribbon from the corsage. The lid of the box is sealed and finished in the same way as the florist's box.

Once again, I should remind you that very few flowers that have been used for special occasions will come out of the sand in good condition. Some may simply fall apart. If they do, take some of the petals and a few other parts of the flowers and greenery and glue them to a white, uncoated paper plate, imitating a little flower or a small bouquet. Glue rick-rack or an appropriate braid around the edge of the plate. Add a ribbon loop to the back of the plate in case the owner wants to use it as a hanger.

10. Projects for Children

ONE COLD WINTER'S DAY I took my four-and-a-half-year-old granddaughter to lunch. As we talked about what we would do in the afternoon — there must always be something planned to share on grandmother's day — I suggested to little Kathy that this would be a fine time to learn how to dry flowers.

Right after lunch we went to the florist's shop, where we spent a lovely springlike half hour amid the sights and scents of his wares. Finally, we settled on one light pink carnation and one perfect, deep pink sweetheart rose. (Pink is a good choice because the color dries so well.)

At home, I put my little flower dryer on a chair in front of the card table and spread some newspaper on the floor to catch the spills. I put out the equipment she would need and also the appropriate photographs used in this book. After showing her where to begin, I let her go ahead on her own. I think this freedom improved her concentration; I had to make suggestions in only a couple of instances. When the two flowers were covered with sand, I marked the boxes and we put them on a shelf to dry.

On our next day together, about two weeks later, the first thing Kathy wanted to do was look at her flowers. I let her hold the box while I, in turn, held her hands to steady the flow of sand from her treasures. As she saw them emerge, she wanted to know, "Are they still alive?"

Teaching a child to dry flowers is more than a pleasurable pastime for both of you; it is an excellent way to open young eyes to the fascinating world of nature. The very fact that you have to study the form and details of a flower to know how it should look when it is dry teaches a good deal about the conformation of flowers. If you name the parts of the flower as you go along, the child will learn as he plays.

For a child as young as four or five, all of the materials and equipment should be scaled down to his size and ability — a small box or pail of sand, small boxes to hold the flowers, even a smaller-than-usual paper cup to use as the pouring vessel. The flowers should be dried with the stems attached, since the final bouquet will not need much manipulation of the stems.

I wish I could suggest that you have the child pick a few dandelions for his first project, but I can't because,

try as I may, I have never been able to keep the heads on dandelions after they have been dried — they fall apart or shrivel up. A good substitute, though, are the common pink or white clovers. Let your child pick five or six of these to lay on a small bed of sand in his drying box. Show him how to pour the sand around the flower heads, making sure that the stems are covered too. At the same time, in another box, let him dry some clover leaves. These stay a nice bright green and will make his bouquet look lovely and lifelike. Label the boxes and show him where to store them on a closet shelf. Make him promise not to disturb the boxes until you look at them together. To be safe, wait at least five days from the time he has put them to bed.

This is enough serious "work" for a young child, but in a day or so help him collect a few airy weeds (some may even have minute flowers on them) to use as filler. These will be air-dried, so show him how to wrap the ends with a pipe cleaner and hang the bunch to dry in a dark corner. A damp basement, you'll remember, is not a good place for drying flowers. The filler will be ready to use by the time the clover and leaves are dried.

When the big day comes to uncover the buried treasure and make the bouquet, be prepared with a small pottery or metal vase, which your child can fill with sand. Pouring the sand off the flowers and leaves must be done gently, so put your hands over your child's and guide him as he pours. This is a good time and place to teach a child gentleness.

Have him carefully lay the flowers and the leaves, along with the filler, on a piece of plain paper so he can see what he has to work with. Now let him proceed to place all of the material as he wishes into the little vase. Once again, he must be very, very gentle. But if, by chance, he isn't quite gentle enough, or the flowers are exceptionally fragile, you can still save the day. Take a small salt dish or jar lid, or any container that is small and shallow, and fill it with sand. Lay the little flower heads on top of the sand, put the clover leaves around them, and fill in with the tops of the weeds so that no sand shows. Voilà! A creation!

I've chosen very simple flowers for this example and you'll be surprised how charming they can be. Do try any you wish but be sure they are the kind that dry well and don't take too long either to cover with sand or to dry, as a small child may lose interest.

The sweetheart rose is a good winter's choice, and most florists have them in stock all season. If you buy half a dozen, your child can dry one or two and you can do the rest; they are always handy to have around. Use the instructions for drying zinnias, and leave the foliage on the flower. The clear pink roses keep their color well; *don't* buy the new variety that has a green vein in the outside petal.

Flower-drying is a good nature-study project for Brownie or Girl Scout troops or any small group of children. Although eventually the youngsters should be encouraged to collect their own flowers, if they live in an area where this is possible, I strongly suggest that the leader supply the flowers for the first session. In this way it is possible to control the method and the drying time for the flowers. Ask each child to bring a shoe box to the meeting. The sand, paper cups, cardboard, and scissors may be supplied by the leader.

Be sure that each child's box is marked with the flower, the date, and the owner's name. Put the boxes in a corner or closet where they will not be disturbed until you are ready to hold another session, at which time the youngsters should be asked to bring a small vase or container. Because sand won't burn the drying flowers, you can afford to be flexible about the date of the next meeting. Just be sure you allow enough time for everything to dry completely.

When you show the children how to pour the sand off their flowers, please impress upon them that no matter how "alive" the flowers look, they are now extremely brittle and must be handled very gently. Have a sand-filled paper cup for each child to put his dried flowers in after uncovering them and before arranging them in his vase. This will prevent accidents, while at the same time giving the children a chance to see how their bouquets will look before they are finally arranged.

11. Experimenting Is Fun

MOST of what I have learned about drying flowers — which dry well and which lose their color or fall apart — has been the result of experimenting. Part of the enjoyment of this hobby is in the element of mystery about what will emerge from beneath the sand. Once you have learned the basic techniques, I hope you will try your hand at drying anything that strikes your fancy. You may end up with a bunch of shattered flowers, but you may also shatter some rules in the process and come up with your own creative new ways of using dried floral material.

Take something as simple as parsley. Although it seems an unlikely subject for flower arranging, we had several months of pleasure last winter from two large bunches of curly green parsley that I brought home from the supermarket with the groceries.

If you would like to duplicate my experiment, cut the stems to about two or three inches in length and dry each sprig upright in sand according to the directions in Chapter 7. You can dry quite a few pieces in one shoe box; the dried sprigs are fairly strong and don't fall apart easily.

I put my dried parsley in an old blue and white crockery bowl, filled to within an inch of the top with dry sand. I stuck the sprigs in the sand until nothing was visible but the parsley. Since it was December, I decided to make the arrangement look seasonal by impaling bright red cranberries on toothpicks and poking them here and there among the parsley greens. The bouquet sat on the breakfast room table until it was time to replace it with holly and the more traditional Christmas greens, then I removed the cranberries and put the bowl of parsley in a cupboard.

Late in January, I brought it out again. This time I stuck some small dried marigolds among the sprigs. The parsley kept its color for almost a year and served as the background greenery for several other flower arrangements.

Many of my experiments, I realize, take place in late fall and winter. On the one hand, I suppose, I am trying to prolong the flower season, and on the other to recapture its pleasures during the cold months when one cannot enjoy flowers in the garden or the fresh bouquets that are sold on city street corners in spring and summer. How much pleasanter to dry the last roses of summer instead of leaving them to blacken in the frost, or even to live for a day or two in the house! (The last roses, incidentally, dry very well indeed.)

Last fall when I was in a hurry and there were still some lovely globe amaranths in the garden, I took a little basket and filled it with the amaranths as if I were making an arrangement for the table. Instead of putting them in water or even taking the time to dry them in sand or hang them by the traditional method for air drying, I simply hung the whole basket from a wire from the attic ceiling. The amaranths dried beautifully with the heads all erect. When they were dry, I tucked in a little dried greenery and my arrangement was complete. The reason I hung the basket, instead of simply putting it on a table, is because mice adore this flower and would have a feast if they could get at it in an undisturbed place such as an attic.

Winter is a good time to experiment with florist's flowers, some of which dry much better than the same flowers picked from a garden. If you get an arrangement as a gift, take a few flowers out of the bouquet as soon as you can, to dry them while they are fresh. If the gift was for some special occasion, it is fun to make a miniature dried replica of the fresh arrangement to preserve the memory of the event it celebrated.

One day, as I sat enjoying the beauty and fragrance of a paper-white narcissus growing in an old Delft bowl, I decided to see if I could lengthen the time we could enjoy it. First I cut off the cluster of blossoms, leaving about three inches of stem. I dried the flowers in sand, using the method described for ageratum (Figure 14). I cut off the foliage and put it in a separate box of sand to dry. With a paring knife, I scraped out the inside of the bulb, cutting very carefully until only a shell about one fourth of an inch thick remained. The shell went into a third drying box on a bed of sand. I poured sand into the shell and all around it until the bulb was completely covered. It took about two weeks for the bulb to dry, but this would vary with the size of the bulb and the thickness of the shell.

Everything came out fine except for the foliage, which was yellow and ugly, but provided me with a good excuse to visit several florists (where I picked up a number of ideas about other flowers and greens to dry during the winter). And at one shop I discovered the emerald commodor palm with long stiff leaves attached to a central stem. I dried a few of the longer ones, which made an excellent substitute for the natural leaves of the narcissus.

Then came the fun of assembling the flowering bulb. First I filled the cavity of the bulb with floral clay, as a way of holding the whole composition in place. Then I put it in a flower bowl filled with sand, burying it to a depth of two thirds of the bulb. This steadied the arrangement as I worked and held it steady when it was completed.

Next, I attached a wire stem to the three inches of

natural stem I had left on the blossoms, covered the stem with florist's tape, and stuck it into the clay. The substitute leaves were stiff enough to put in the clay without any wire attachments.

The dried narcissus made a charming, and most unusual, floral piece for an end table or coffee table, and "bloomed" for the rest of the winter!

12. Save the Pieces

NOT EVERY FLOWER or branch of foliage that you dry will come out of the sand intact. Even some successes will drop a few flowerets in the drying process. Don't throw these away; store them in an odds-and-ends box — you'll find dozens of uses for them. One of my favorites is to make a dried-flower candle.

For this project, any ten-inch smooth candle will do. Insert the candle very securely into its holder, using a bit of floral clay at the bottom to hold it firmly in place.

The other materials you will need are:

a pair of tweezers   aluminum foil
a toothpick   Elmer's glue

Make a small pan, about four inches in diameter, from the foil and pour a little glue into it.

Start decorating your candle from the bottom at the point where it emerges from the holder. You can use three or four flowers, about one-half inch in diameter, or a row of sturdy green leaves, such as individual box-wood leaves or the tips of leatherleaf fern, to make a base. Single flowerets of green hydrangea are also excellent, and much less delicate to work with than they look.

Use one, two, or even three rows of this material for the base. As you continue up the candle, graduate the size of the flowers and the flowerets, ending about two inches from the wick end of the candle with the very tiniest of all. You can either cover the candle completely, placing one flower against the next, or space them to let the candle itself show through. Whichever style you choose, do apply the flowers at random, without any set pattern. The look you want is a drift of flowers. If you do a pair of candles, use the same flowers and greenery, but don't attempt to place the materials in exactly the same formation.

To attach the flowers:

Pick up the sturdy flowers, like the zinnia heads, with your hand and apply a spot of glue with the toothpick to the base of the flower. Hold the flower gently against the candle until it begins to stick — it doesn't take long.

Use your tweezers to pick up the delicate flowers. Dip them in glue and hold them against the candle. This is a bit tricky but you'll soon get on to it. Dainty flowers, such as larkspur heads, individual ageratum flowerets, tiny coralbells, and other very light pieces, will stick to the candle almost immediately.

Obviously, these candles are not for burning. But they make most attractive decorative accents on a dining room table, perhaps on either side of a green house plant, or on end tables, or in a guest room. The candles may be kept on display even in humid weather, since whatever wilting takes place doesn't seem to show.

Although you can use any kinds of small flowers and bits and pieces of flowers that you have on hand, here are some that are particularly good:

Tiny rosebuds, zinnias, and marigolds

The flowerets of forget-me-nots, coralbells, larkspur, hydrangeas, and ageratum

Table decorations for church luncheons or suppers, or any similar large affair, are often a problem, especially when it is impractical (as it so often is) to buy fresh flowers out of season. Here your imagination, some inexpensive construction paper, and your odds-and-ends box can come to the rescue.

To make centerpieces for individual tables, cut the construction paper into round or oblong mats. Put a candle holder in the center and glue a nosegay or other arrangement of dried flower bits and pieces to the mat. Finish it off if you like with a ribbon bow. (And if you have a speaker's table or other head table, do try using a dried-flower arrangement instead of fresh flowers, to coordinate the theme.)

Dried-flower-decorated place mats are lovely for any

kind of party, and especially fun to create for all holiday affairs and such days as Valentine's Day, Saint Patrick's Day, or harvest-day festivals.

Instead of buying expensive gift-package decorations, why not use the contents of your odds-and-ends box to dress up your gift packages? Once you start seeing the possibilities, you are sure to find a dozen ways of your own to create lovely gifts or decorations with pieces of dried materials.

If you have a really big supply of "disasters," you might consider the idea of approaching the program chairman of your local senior citizens' center, which is always looking for new handmade bazaar items, or the occupational therapists and directors of schools and homes for the aged or handicapped. From such simple beginnings, may come more ambitious efforts. How gratifying it would be to teach the craft of drying and preserving flowers to those not fortunate enough to be able to go out for themselves to see the beauty in the world. If this is not a project you feel equipped to take on yourself, why not suggest it to the program chairman of your local garden club?

This may seem a long way from the suggestions for using your pieces of broken flowers. If so, it is typical of what you can expect once you become involved in the fine (but easy) art of drying flowers in the natural elements of sand and air.